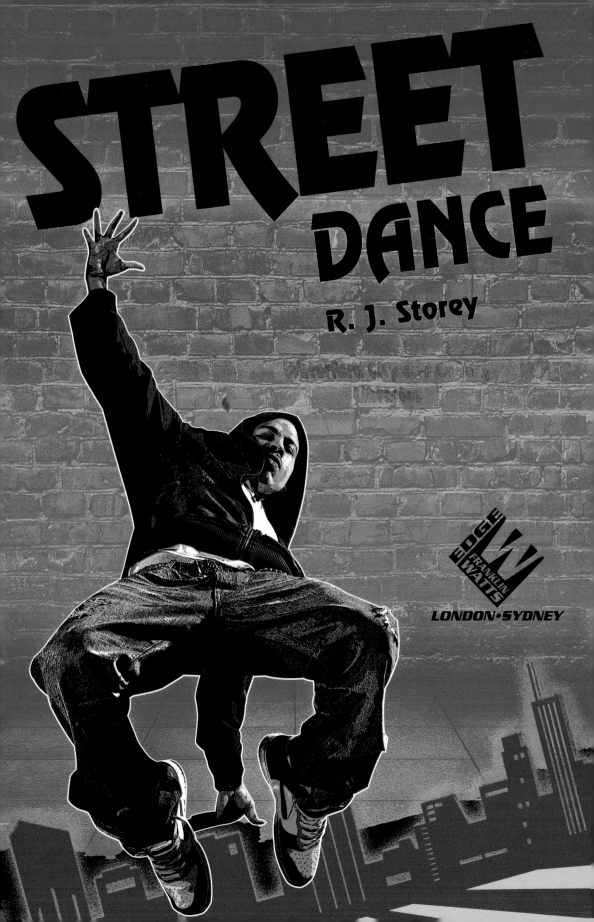

STREET
DANCE

R. J. Storey

EDGE
FRANKLIN WATTS

LONDON·SYDNEY

To watch some great street dance videos, scan the QR codes with your smartphone. See pages 9, 11, 12, 19 and 21.

First published in 2013 by
Franklin Watts
338 Euston Road
London NW1 3BH

Franklin Watts Australia
Level 17/207 Kent Street
Sydney NSW 2000

Series editor: Adrian Cole

Packaged for Franklin Watts by Storeybooks
rita@storeybooks.co.uk
Designer: Rita Storey

A CIP catalogue record for this book is available
from the British Library.

Printed in China

Dewey classification: 793.3

ISBN
(HB): 978 1 4451 1946 5
(Library ebook): 978 1 4451 2586 2

Franklin Watts is a division of Hachette Children's Books,
an Hachette UK company
www.hachette.co.uk

Photo acknowledgements
AFP/Getty Images: 8 – 9. Getty Images: 10.
Poison/robynjanephotography: 20 – 21.
Prodance 11 and 19. Redferns via Getty
Images: 18 – 19. Shutterstock: 1, 3, 4, 5, 6, 7,
12, 13, 14, 15, 16, 17 and 22.

Every attempt has been made to clear copyright.
Should there be any inadvertent omission, please
apply to the Publishers for rectification.

Contents

Street Dance

Street dance began in clubs and on the streets.

Since it began street dance has been performed to all types of urban music.

"Find your street dance style."

There are many styles of street dance. Each one has its own identity.

Breakdance

Breakdancing is a style of street dance done to hip-hop and funk music.

A breakdance starts with a stand up dance move called toprock.

Toprock is followed by floor moves called downrock.

Toprock, six-step and baby freeze are the basic breakdance moves.

Dance Battles

A team of breakdancers is called a crew.

Crews battle it out to see who has the best moves.

A "dance-off" between good crews is awesome to watch.

This crew called *Jinjo* won the b-boy Championship World Finals in 2012.

b-boy & b-girl

Breakdancers are called breakers, b-boys or b-girls.

Morris is an American b-boy World Champion.

Roxy was a trampolinist before she became a b-girl.

Power Moves

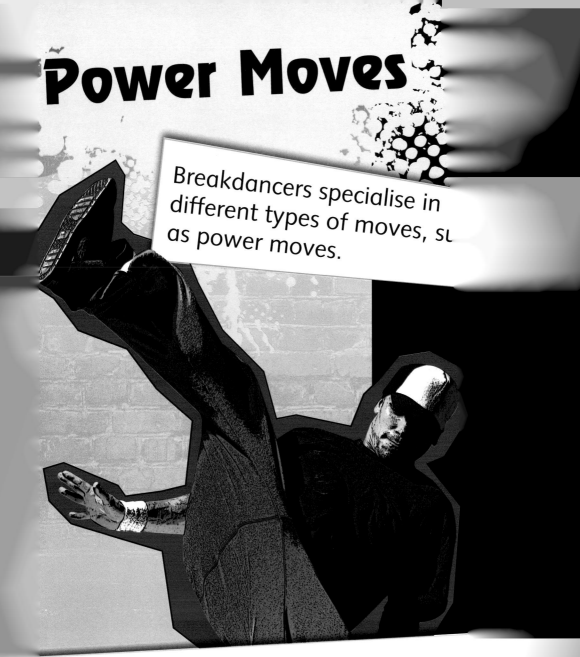

Breakdancers specialise in different types of moves, su as power moves.

Power moves are normally spinning moves. These need power and technique.

"Using a fresh new move is a good way to win a battle."

Spins on the hands or the head are dramatic to watch.

Freezes

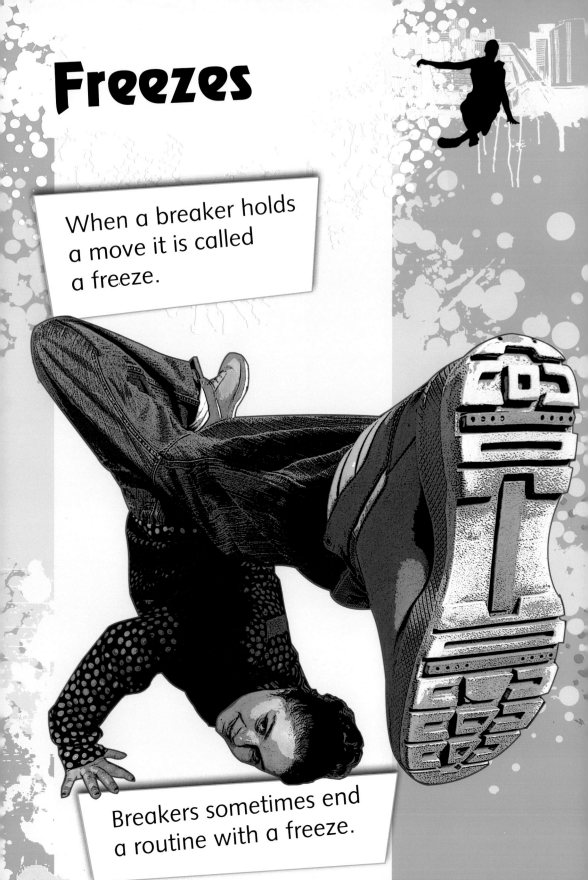

When a breaker holds a move it is called a freeze.

Breakers sometimes end a routine with a freeze.

Drops

The move between toprock and downrock is a drop.

Your Style

New street dance styles are being created all the time.

In dance schools, street dance is often taught through routines.

Poppin' & Lockin'

Poppin' is a street dance created in the 1970s. Poppin' is the tensing and relaxing of your muscles to the beat of the music.

Lockin' is a funky dance created by Don Campbell and his group *The Lockers*.

Being Famous

As well as dance battles, there are lots of other ways in which street dancers can compete with each other.

Talent shows feature street dancers and dance crews. Crews like *Diversity* and *Flawless* have brought street dance onto mainstream TV.

Street dancers can get to be film stars too!

Brooke is part of a crew called *Plague*. He danced in the film *Streetdance 3D*.

Competitions

Street dancers from dance schools all over the world get together to dance in competitions.

This dance crew, called *Poison*, are UDO over 18 World Champions.

"High heels, high hopes!"

Poison

Christabelle is the choreographer for *Poison*. She arranges some wicked moves.

Poison were semi-finalists on Got To Dance 2013.

Just Dance

"Street dance is not just throwing down and making moves. You gotta feel it."

"Don't care, just move."

"Dance for yourself no one else matters."

Glossary

baby freeze A freeze held with one knee resting on the opposite elbow.

b-boy A male breakdancer.

b-girl A female breakdancer.

Breakdance A style of street dance done to hip-hop and funk music.

Crew A team of streetdancers.

Dance battles Dance competitions between crews.

Dance-off A competition between two crews. Dancers perform alternately until one crew is declared the winner.

Downrock Floor moves in a breakdance.

Drops The moves between toprock and downrock in breakdancing.

Freezes Breakdance moves that are held motionless.

Funk music A style of music used to breakdance to.

Hip-hop An urban youth culture that covers MCing, rapping, b-boying and grafitti art.

Poppin' A style of street dance in which dancers tense and relax their muscles to the beat of the music.

Power moves Dramatic street dance moves.

Six-step A breakdance move with six steps. It is one of the basic breakdance moves.

Street dance Dance styles that evolved outside of dance studios.

Toprock A stand up dance move in breakdancing.

UDO (United Dance Organisation) A company which stages street dance events.

Urban Relating to a town or city.

To watch some great street dance in action, scan the QR codes on these pages or copy the links below into your browser.

9   http://www.youtube.com/watch?v=QOhk3ja6mUY

11   http://www.youtube.com/watch?v=r3HU080TJSE

12   http://www.youtube.com/watch?v=LvRrBdKbwk8

19   http://www.youtube.com/watch?v=9ha0SuymVWo

21   http://www.youtube.com/watch?v=EjzGK9D7Yyc

Index

Websites

www.udostreetdance.com/events/worlds2013
Get involved in street dance through a dance
school near you.

www.streetdanceinternational.com
The official streetdance international website.

http://bboychampionships.com/
The official site for the b-boy and b-girl World
Championships.

Please note: every effort has been made by
the Publishers to ensure that the websites in
this book contain no inappropriate or offensive
material. However, because of the nature of
the Internet, it is impossible to guarantee that
the contents of these sites will not be altered.
We strongly advise that Internet access is
supervised by a responsible adult.

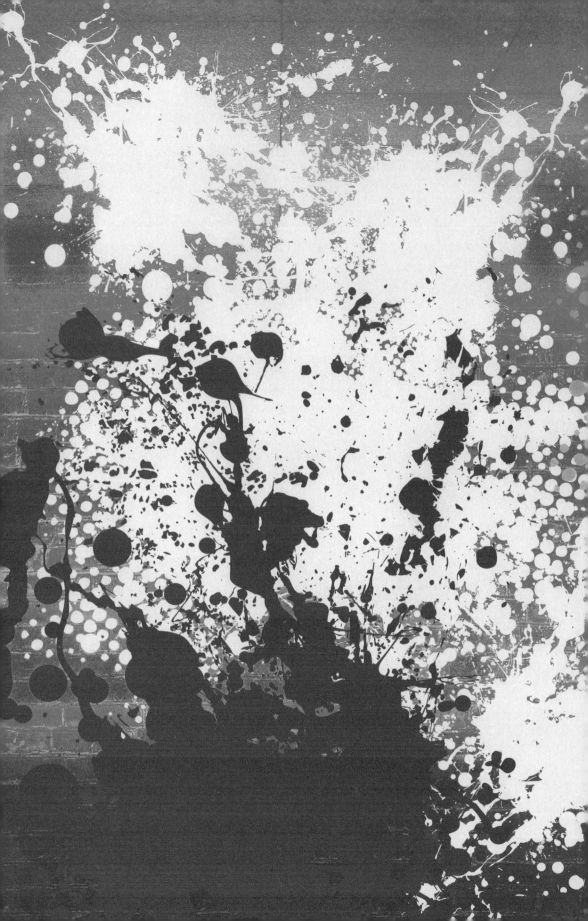